Secretz
& other free verse poems
by Elliot M. Rubin

secretz
and
other free verse poems
by
Elliot M. Rubin

Copyright December 2020
Library of Congress

ISBN # 978-1-7363641-1-6

No part of this book may be reproduced in any form whatsoever without the author's prior express written consent.

This book is fiction, and all names, people, places, and happenings are from the author's imagination and are used fictionally.

Any resemblance to any living or dead persons and/or businesses, locations, or events is coincidental in its entirety.

All rights reserved

Dedication
To my grandchildren
Shane, Isabelle, Jonathan, Carter,
Alexandra, Melanie, Mollie, and Madison

In memory of my father
Herman S. Rubin
who wrote poetry all his life

I believe poetry is to be read and understood by all. It needs to be written in plain language for everyone's enjoyment.

Too often, poets write in-depth, penetrating poems where you need to be well-read and/or versed in literature's nuances to appreciate the poetry, not this book or any of my writings. I try to write so everyone can enjoy a few moments of intellectual satisfaction without consulting a dictionary or encyclopedia.

Table of Contents

secretz	7
tuesday - secretz II	8
indiana family values - secretz III	9
muse wanted, apply within - secretz IV	10
a married woman	11
american heroes	12
thompson park	13
a funeral	14
hyphen-love	15
love conquer$ all	16
school	17
holy tree	18
viewpoint	19
that night	20
facing facts	21
pandemic slice of life 2020	22
friendship pointer	24
circle of life	25
a fix	26
the old stag	27
dinner at the plaza hotel, n.y.c.	28
freedom	29
colors	30
rings	31

small cuts	32
realization	33
driving	34
jealousy	35
driving for love	36
the shower	37
sounds of love	38
winter wind	39
holiday memories	40
lips	41
flowers	42
old new friends	44
backseat	45
carwash afternoon	46
performing	47
night hunters	48
self-recognition	49
enough	50
realization of age	51
early morning blues	52
papers	53
once upon a time on Christmas eve	54
BIG OT	56
a modern romance	57

life in manhattan .... **Error! Bookmark not defined.**

for-ever 59

occupied 60

celebrating 61

secretz I

enthralled with her,
wishing for a love that mirrors
romeo and juliet, except her love
is for another, as cyrano learned

she is his muse,
the prompt for his poems,
inspiration for his craft,
the love of his life
unknowingly
breaking his heart

for years she never realizes

the world reads of his love for her
in books and magazines, yet he never
tells her except in writing for others

until one day
by accident
she reads of it

then realizes
the poems
are for her

tuesday - secretz II

after finishing,
he rolls a blunt
then dozes off-
wakes up later
the crumbled sheets
are still warm
where she had been,
empty now-
the pillow is still creased
by an impression
her face so willing to offer a kiss,
a smile, words of endearment-
remaining strands of hair,
lipstick stains,
the scent of passion
still lingers; tells of the earlier tryst-
he didn't hear her leave
she is missed already-
the gift left on the dresser
is also gone-
he can't wait
till next tuesday afternoon
as they've done for years,
while their spouses
are at work

indiana family values - secretz III

located off the main street
no name on the door, just a number,
the place is wall to wall with women-
standing at the end of the bar
a cigarette dramatically inhaled
by a long-haired blond pillow princess
dressed in black tights
with a sheer pink blouse
who looks straight ahead,
staring in the bar back mirror
while she slowly exhales
pointing down at a shot glass

the topless bartender with no makeup,
half her head shaved with a full-color
sleeve of tats from wrist to shoulder
walks over to fill it again,
leans over to kiss the woman
staking her out for others to see

on the dance floor, girls are slow dancing,
grinding on one another, kissing,
making plans for after closing

this bar has political protection
while other gay bars in this midwestern city
have been raided and closed-
sitting in a dark corner booth with a young
nineteen-year-old girl is the mayor's wife,
recruiting for a threesome with him

muse wanted, apply within - secretz IV

the blank sheet of paper
stares back, unblinking,
waiting for creativity to burst forth
to write words of poetry

unknown to the paper
it will need to wait
since my muse left me
for a more stable life

late nights of writing
were way too much for her-
sleep-deprived, she walks out
upset; all i wrote about was her

i placed an ad to replace her
to try to recapture the magic
but a muse is hard to find;
my paper still remains blank

a married woman

everyone who saw her
admired the fair skin,
smooth complexion
no marks, no imperfections

gentle hands with a soft touch,
eyes filled with empathy
ears open to hear sorrows,
lips never speaking ill

perfect beyond compare
completely scarless
until you look inside
after years of verbal abuse

in a loveless marriage
trapped with kids,
too timid to escape

until one day she did

american heroes

they never die
when a righteous cause
comes along-
they rear their head
charging into the wrong,
ignore warnings to be still-
beaten with clubs,
jailed, shot, spit at,
injuries sustained
they stand up
when others won't,
though death
eventually
takes their bodies-
heroes live on
  urging us to fight

when we need them
  their spirit is with us

miss you,
Abby Hoffman
Elijah Cummings

thompson park

the county park down the road
is open, filled with individuals;
lonely joggers, single mothers pushing strollers,
seniors sitting by themselves
watching clouds roll softly overhead

a small lake is filled with fish-
groups of families at the beach,
docks filled with rowboats for
lovers and friends to take on the water,
along with groups of teens
swimming with their sweethearts
in the heat of a long, hot, summer's day
are nowhere to be seen

only memories remain
of the towns swimming hole,
where everyone knew everyone-
the beach is closed, docks gone,
polluted water, no swimming-
now it's a bustling county park
filled with individuals

a funeral

i read he died

the funeral was last week
no one attended
not surprised;
bastards don't get mourners,
flowers or tears

wish i was there
to throw dirt
on his coffin-
to make sure
he is dead;
then go out for a beer

hyphen-love

our love is like a hyphen

separate yet attached

together yet apart

we be-long

to-gether

for-ever

love conquer$ all

repulsed by his sweaty hands
she refused to hold them
as they walk side by side
on their first date

she said her hands are cold
so they are kept in her side
jacket pockets as they strolled,
making meaningless small talk

after a while,
he asks if she needs a lift home.
he dials his car to pick her up;
a chauffeured Bentley drives up
as he offers his sweaty palm
to ease her into the car

"would you like to join me?" she asks

seems love can overcome di$gust

school

as neighbors, he was fourteen
when they met, she sixteen;
one summer day, they hit it
off at the beach and kissed

days flew by, vacation over,
school starts soon but not needed-
she gave him an education
he will never forget

holy tree

the forest
is packed tight
tree to tree,
a lush green canopy
blocks the sun,
stunts the growth
of smaller trees below

every december
the taller ones are culled,
designated for display,
to be dressed in garland,
tinsel and colorful hanging balls;
while smaller, less full trees
are donated to people in need

no glitter or shiny things
hang on those trees,
just family pictures,
and personal trinkets,

viewpoint

i discovered girls
at thirteen

my parents
invited friends
to our home

sneaking a peek
i said to myself
*"who wants to sleep
with forty-year-old women?"*

at seventy-five,

sixty-year-old girls are sexy,
forty-year-olds could kill me,
younger ones are suicidal

that night

a run-down summer cottage

old floral linoleum scuffed bare from wear

midnight dark, only the moon lights the room

unmade mattress smells musty;
    no sheets, no pillows

at sixteen, we were in heaven, love, lust, passion-

decades later

i still smell her perfume when i think back,
feel her skin on my tongue,
her arms wrapped around my neck

the emotions i felt that night never leave

though she did

facing facts

while my mind
is seventeen
my body arrived
at seventy-five

things i want to do
feel i can
are all in the past

the will is still there
urges me on
unfortunately
nature physically stops me

only in my mind
am i still capable

pandemic slice of life 2020

the sun went down hours ago-
i'm alone now,
the girl left after i paid her;
she was nothing great just the usual stuff-
sitting in the dark
the glare of the street light
through the window helps

pour some whisky-
  i prefer to drink alone,
    the amber drug
      seems to fill the glass
        in slow motion

i'm in no rush
i sip, taste it
the burn goes down, warm
it rushes to numb
my senses,
my life,
my miserable
lonely life

ended up
in this rented room
after losing my job,
career in ruins

the roach in the room

    stops

not moving when it sees me-

truth is i don't care;
let it climb down
                my
                    wall,
eat the scraps i dropped-
we are alike in many ways;
we both scurry to survive,
no future,
no hope,
just live in the present

at least the bottle still has some left

friendship pointer

her pointer was still very sharp
after many years of use-
able to single out the minutia
in every conversation
or book it was into-
but with time
became blunted,
almost dull,
not able to find its place
or read anymore
due to stroke,
complications
beyond its control

but i understand

i still keep it
to say hello
now and then,
in my honored
friendship drawer

circle of life

sardines are similar
to many people,
they swim around
in a world of ocean
where they go in circles-
they fall to a deep bottom,
sometimes above or out
where they should never go-
once born, they are
alone in the sea,
left by their mother
with no guidance,
unless they stay
in a school;
part of the crowd,
indistinguishable,
an individual
chugging along
or swallowed up
by a bigger fish
ending their journey-
never attaining,
only living-
just another fish
amongst many

a fix

yesterday she flew high,
   unstoppable powder,
      felt unbound strength all-day
         but that was yesterday

today is today,
positive powder
is gone,
all used up,
now back to normal

her time is spent
looking for him,
needing another
short snort or two

looking 'round
not to be
found, he's gone,
arrested

crashing,
sweating,
bad chills,
tired

down,
sad,
brain
drain

cocaine

the old stag

the verdant forest
silently rolls
over mountains
for miles and miles,
filling valleys
with a tree-topped canopy
while the tranquility of quiet
is torn asunder
in the thickets below-
a pack of wolves
attack an old stag
with its massive rack
of pointed antlers
it circles 'round
defending itself,
thrashes about,
tears at its hungry attackers
fighting for life,
they for their meal

in a treed city
pocket park
an elderly man
uses his wooden cane
to defend himself
from three teens,
intent on theft
to feed a drug habit

animals live everywhere

dinner at the plaza hotel, n.y.c.

one night, with friends,
we dined at the plaza hotel
when i notice a woman
at the table next to ours

a cocktail is gently placed
in front of her, served correctly,
not too far nor too close,
within a short reach from the edge

long, delicate fingers with a french
manicure stretch out, wrapping
around the glass, lifting it ever so
lightly to her lips; the olive never shifts

strands of fine pearls loop around
her neck, casually resting
on an elegant black silk blouse,
set off by perfect, blemish-free skin

her scintillating floral scent slices
through my entrée's aroma-
she appears soft, delicate, fragile;
sitting there, she stands out

truthfully, i would rather an earthy
beer girl with tats who can
tell a bawdy joke or two,
then a porcelain doll in my arms

freedom

on special days
people give presents
wrapped in fancy paper and ribbon-
gifts that take many forms,
not always neat and tidy

as time goes on
they tend to wear thin,
outlasting their usefulness;
but his last gift
was the best one yet

he is yelling,
in anger, he threw car keys
at her head

she caught them

stops at the bank
cleans out the account;
drives away, singing,
heading nowhere
far away

she loves the gift of safety

colors

the first time i saw you
my face turned green
with envy; i wish i was
the person you were with

after we started to date
i was red with jealousy
when at a party you
smiled at other people

many times you would
flash yellow feelings to
calm me down, be cautious,
i loved you too much

i will never forget
the day you walked out
of my life; i feel so blue
without you in my arms

my life is now colorless

rings

it sits on the night table
next to his bed, round, gold,
quite thin for a wedding ring-
not a thick flashy symbol,
just a slim round reminder

it never came off his finger
for almost sixty years,
until today-
each slight scratch on the ring
tells a story in his life

it saw happy times as well as sad,
births of children,
a death of one too -
it saw a war in Asia with him,
always there, a reminder of her

now, after he passed, his daughter
holds the ring as she reaches up
to open the chain around her neck,
places the ring on the necklace
as it slides down next to his wife's

now they are together again

small cuts

tiny parallel lines
slice her forearm,
release a flood
of feelings
as blood
trickles out,
curving
down her wrist
as tears well up
waiting to flow

undressed,
looking out a window
the sun is bright,
white cotton-puffs
drift by
as storm clouds
twirl in her mind

resting on the bed
she turns her face
to the nightstand,
to an open vial
of sleeping pills

waiting to be taken

realization

they stood
battalion firm,
thick,
virile,
upright,
massive
until one by one,
they fell aside-
no longer together
but fluid as sand,
exposing
firmament below
for all to see

at seventy-five,
i miss my hair

driving

on calm
sunny days
driving along
winding country roads
without a care
in the world

i always seem to think of you

every intersection
with a stop sign
signals my heart
to tear a little more,
as i remember
the day you left

ignored my pleas
to stop!
stay,
start over

i screwed up
not loving you

enough

jealousy

every time i start my car
i hear the motor roar to life,
pistons jumping up and down
awash in lubricating oil

if any part of my car breaks
it can be replaced
at the auto parts store
down the road a bit

my knee has arthritis,
my kidneys don't function well
my eyes need new glasses every year
my appendix burst years ago

hearing is not so great
i fractured a femur
    plus my right heel,
not even mentioning
impacted wisdom teeth

i am jealous of my car,
where is the parts store
for my body?

driving for love

she drove
right into my heart,
foot on the throttle
full speed ahead,
the green light
of love was given-
throwing
her yellow silk dressed
curves at me,
i yielded,
ignored
the red light feelings
i kept noticing,
until she left and
took my dog

that was the stop sign for me

the shower

last night
she came home late,
roosters already up;
a long shower
it was a sensual dinner date
badly needed
hot water
rinses her face
taking off
a lover's kisses;
only memories
are left of the
impressions
pressed on tired lips-
the coldness
of tile feels good
against flushed cheeks,
as a torrent
races down her body
like tiny pinpricks
forcing
last nights scents
down the drain

before bed
she hangs her clothes;
slowly
she smells
the date's sweet lilac perfume
on the blouse

to relive the evening
with her again

sounds of love

a gentle kiss
    of the lips

lovers hug
    say goodbye

two hands
    with fingers entwined

hint of a sigh
    the heart makes
        when you think
            of your dearest

the crinkle
    of tissue paper
        wiping away
            tears of love

all just above a whisper

winter wind

the arctic wind
blows from the north,
last green colors
of summer turn
  deathly red
holding on
  to no avail

autumn is chased
by winter's coming
leaves twist and twirl
fall to their death

winter coats
brought from the closet
  low temps arrive,
as well as children's
snow expectation

soon holiday season
full of gifts to unwrap
is almost upon us

i bundle up
to go outside,
breathing clean air
as ice-cold winds
fiercely blow,
forcing me
to hold my jacket closed

holiday memories

she remembers as a child
father brought her to town
to see holiday lights
strung from lamp posts
and buildings
for the christmas season-
she helped mother
hang decorations
on the tree father fresh cut-
as a young bride
the future looked bright
until it didn't-
blackness descended,
her world turned dark,
wedding vows broken
due to pills and drink-
now in manhattan
she sleeps in a box
on a subway grate
for warmth-
closing her eyes she
remembers yesterdays
as hundreds of feet
walk by her,
invisible to them
as they celebrate
a holiday of good cheer
caring for others

lips

our faces touch

my lips fondle yours

i feel it may be love

time will tell
if true

flowers

sometimes people regret
picking a flower
from the garden

one of many
to select from,
especially the roses;
  graceful,
    colorful,
      attractive to the eyes,
but the thorns
  are prickly,
    hurtful,
they can bring resentment

once the stem is cut
it can't be nourished

love is like that on occasion

similarities

harlots do it
for carnal pleasure

poets write
for self-enjoyment

neither does it
for the money

both can get
recognition of sorts

old new friends

i am making new old friends again

my neighbors
are all seniors
as am i;
we often socialize
until one spouse
becomes ill

we stop going out;
then one day
a black van arrives
to take one away-
after a while
the spouse and live-in aide
sit in the driveway
waving hello

eventually the spouse
becomes frail,
thin,
no longer
walks or sits outside,
soon a black van arrives
once more

i am making new old friends again

backseat

mother's car
wasn't big
yet it sufficed

my needs were met
that summer
many years ago
in the rear seat
with a special girl

if only the car could talk
the tales it would tell

thinking back,
i wonder
where both are
these decades later

carwash afternoon

one sunny afternoon
   waiting
for my car to appear
a short, pudgy,
   teased blond-haired girl
stood next to me
holding a small white dog
against her ample chest

pink blouse stretched tight,
skin-hugging leggings
with telltale sparkle makeup
suggest she is a dancer

her shiny pearl white cadillac
with red leather seats appeared,
out of state license plates
confirm my suspicion
since strippers travel a circuit

we smile at each other,
she asks me to visit her
at a men's club tonight;
she's headlining there

i'll let younger guys
   pay for her lap dances,
i am satisfied
   i guessed her occupation,
i don't need her
   for further gratification

plus, i need my sleep

performing

alone with him
after many years

naked

he sees her beauty
not her scars

her body is here

her heart
elsewhere

acting

night hunters

at sunset, most prepare
their bed for hours of sleep;
unlike the prowlers of the dark
hunting for victims to feed on,
then flying back to dank, humid
bat caves to hang during the day

not her, as she readies lovers
for her nocturnal desires
only stopping when satiated,
exhausted, sleeping till the next night

self-recognition

he thought he owned her
never showed any kindness
took her for granted

she stood and then left
her body was only loaned,
her soul never was

enough

society tells them
to be silent

to keep a
status quo of calm

abused women
shout out

no more
NO more
NO MORE

realization of age

my cousin
was a beatnik
in the fifties,
while i a hippie
in the sixties,
smoke'n and rock'n
with willing girls
till exhausted

time catches up

in my fifties
the ponytail went,
the bones started
creak'n not rock'n
while my hair
waves goodbye

young nubile girls
now succumb
to me, in my poems,
not interested
in old bald men
who live wildly
in their dreams

early morning blues

wish i had a trumpet
so i could play it now,
the 3 am blues would
be such a great tune

up at three in the morning
with nowhere to go,
life in suburbia can be so
dull, while the city jives alive

i hear a rhythm in my mind
so clear and crisp, with a slight
vibrato wailing in my head,
yearning to live, breathe, jump

the early morning blues
comes to me every day,
same time, same tune,
until i go back to bed at five

papers

each year
untold millions
of signed papers
determine the lives
of so many people,
tucked tightly
in a satchel
he carries around,
while looking
for more signers

the devil's handiwork
affects men and women
who wish away
their souls
on an invisible
dotted line,
sealing a bargain
they made,
ignoring
the date
payment is due,
while enjoying
the pleasures
it affords them
until he comes to collect

once upon a time on Christmas eve

Julie and Jon snuggled up
in their beds, blankets up tight
right up to their heads

when they heard a pitter-patter
of tiny feet skittering above,
"maybe it's Santa?"
they both said with true love

with a bang and a bung
they heard bells be rung,
the elves are so frantic
this never happened before

Santa is stuck in the chimney
so tight, with hours to go,
he can't stay here,
he'd be oh so slow

he had stopped for a snack
it filled him right up,
with cookies and milk
he drank from a cup

some elves came down first
they were pushing him up,
while four from above
when they heard a big glup!

they all were so frantic
not knowing what to do
the reindeer were huffing
and shuffling their hoofs,
they were ready to fly;
to bid this home
a heartfelt goodbye

so Julie and Jon
hopped into the sleigh,
they'd finish the route
cause tonight
dear old Santa
was just too big
and stout

after making some rounds
they flew to come back,
Santa had twisted and turned
and slid right back out

this night they'll remember
they delivered the toys,
all wrapped with a bow
to good little girls
and sleeping, small boys

BIG OT

OT is a man of few words,
cigar-chewing till the stub
is almost flat, saturated with saliva,
then spitting on the grass
as he waters his small patch
of front lawn grass;
wearing rolled-up sleeves
on his slightly soiled white tee shirt

growing up in Queens, New York
in a working-class, all-white area,
his world views are local,
barbershop news, pool hall gossip

the baseball bat in his trunk
saw combat in street brawls
when Black Lives Matter marchers
passed through his local turf

his president said they were Antifa
radicals, intent on rioting and mayhem

during the fight, he is stabbed-
a black doctor sews him up,
a black nurse cares for the wound, then
holds his hand when he winces in pain

to him, they were good blacks,
but happy they didn't live nearby,
or go to school with his kids

BIG OT is still a bigot

a modern romance

we met in an online app
where she posed in a scanty
panty and bra, the photos
professionally done

dark, flowing hair with
highlights, makeup
applied with a sensual,
beguiling smile nicely staged

the bond between us
was instant- i knew what she is
searching for
   as she wrote underneath,
her goal a long relationship

alluringly beautiful
she's a wealthy man's arm-candy,
yet we communicated on a deep level-
  we are not meant for each other

plus, my wife would not like it

waiting for dinner

the winter wind bites,
rushing in from the bay
frosting his cheeks
a rosy red, as he walks
next to skyscrapers
in the downtown
financial district-
holding his jacket closed
fringes of his silk scarf
start to fly up-
snow begins to cover
black streets
a frosty sanitizing white-
he looks in an alleyway
a quick movement
next to dumpsters
catch his eye-
looks like a small dog
or cat as it scurries under
a container alongside
a pair of men's legs   extending   out
  from a cardboard box-

short blasts from a car horn
  signals his ride is here-
  thanks the driver
  after he opens the door
  for him to enter-
slowly the limo pulls away
heading uptown to The Plaza
for his dinner appointment,
an unlit Cuban Cohiba cigar
clenched in his teeth,

for-ever

when you said
for-ever
did you mean
eternity
or as long
as today lasts

for-ever has different
meanings
i guess,
for-ever this moment
or for end-less moments

once you say for-ever
it will live on in my mind
to the end of my time

though maybe not yours

occupied

so many things
 in life are occupied

the seat
 on the train or bus

the desk
 in school, you wanted

the restroom
 when you need to go

      or

space in someone's heart
 you wanted to fill

celebrating

holidays are cheerful,
smiles,
hugs from loved ones
unless you're alone

the single malt bottle of whisky
is still full this morning,
no one to join
hoisting the jigger
wishing well,
except in a memory

winter winds
blast outside,
snow drifts high
against the door,
he can't leave
they can't enter,
even if they
weren't dead
and buried
years ago

survival of the fittest
or luckiest,
he doesn't know-
maybe it's karma
working its magic,
for how he led his life

the end

I want to thank my Friday Zoom Poetry Critique Group for their help in editing this book: Bill, Carol, David, Rich, Sue, Asha, and Rodney

www.ingramcontent.com/pod-product-compliance
Lightning Source LLC
Chambersburg PA
CBHW060857050426
42453CB00008B/1003